A GIFT FOR:

FROM:

Playing THE GAME · Inspiration _for_ LIFE _and_ GOLF

www.jcountryman.com

www.hallmark.com

Designed by Koechel Peterson & Associates, Minneapolis, MN

Photography by Koechel Peterson & Associates

Thanks to:
The Tournament Players Club, Ponte Vedra Beach, FL
ProLine Golf Corporation, Houston, TX

ISBN: 08499-9574-4 (Hallmark edition)

Printed and bound in China

TABLE *of* CONTENTS

SCOTT SIMPSON

Scott Simpson

Has been a member of the

PGA tour for 10 years.

My biggest thrill and greatest accomplishment in golf was edging Tom Watson by a stroke and winning the 1987 U.S. Open at the Olympic Club. One of my greatest disappointments was having a two-shot lead with three holes to go, twice, before losing a playoff in the 1991 U.S. Open at Hazeltine. Even though the final results were certainly different, I experienced contentment knowing that win or lose I had done my best. I really believe that our attitudes and actions are much more important to God than coming out on top. One of my favorite verses for golf and for life is Colossians 3:17, "Whatever you do in word or deed, do everything in the name of the Lord Jesus, giving thanks to God the Father through Him."

Doing my best on the golf course means developing consistency and paying attention to the little things. One reason I have the reputation of playing well in U.S. Opens and on the harder courses is that I have learned "course management." Hogan, Nicklaus, and Irwin are a few champions who have excelled at course management. To me that means analyzing the course and making wise choices about whether to play it safe or to go for the pin. Before I hit a shot I have to look at my "yardage book" and all the variables such as hazards, wind, lie, and stance before I pick my club and the type of shot. I also have to keep myself relaxed, focus on the shot, and put any distractions out of my mind.

Our situation in life is similar. God has given us His "yardage book," the Bible, to help us. No matter what situation we face, we can turn to this book for wisdom in managing ourselves and our "game." We know there are hazards to avoid, and God gives us the means to focus on what is right and then to make wise decisions. By following His Word, we can do our best for Him, others, and ourselves. Inevitably we all mess up with bad choices or just bad bounces. But by turning back to God, we can take comfort that He will forgive us and we will have more holes to turn things back around.

In *Playing the Game,* Wally and Jim vividly illustrate many of the parallels between golf and life. Through this unique book, they have given golfers and nongolfers alike an opportunity to learn from "18 holes of inspiration" for the course of life and golf. On every hole you will gain wisdom and encouragement from the Bible and also from some of the greatest golf professionals.

In life and golf there is always more to learn; we never master the game. We can always improve no matter what our skill level, and even in a bad round we can always hit at least one shot that will give us hope for next time. One of the great things about life and golf is that they are always challenging—and that's a lot of the fun.

Whether you are a golf pro or just beginning to play, I know you will find wisdom and inspiration from this book. No matter what situations you encounter, your course management will improve as you play the game of golf and live the game of life. When we're done with our round, we sign and turn in our scorecard. I know if you take this book to heart, you will be prepared to shoot the round of your life!

Scott Simpson

SCOTT SIMPSON, *March 1998*

PREFACE

The overwhelming success of our book, *In His Grip: Foundations for Life and Golf,* has clearly revealed a great interest in the parallels between the game of golf and life. People are eager to learn to play better golf, and they are eager to grow in faith.

Eric Prain, in his timeless classic, *Live Hands,* recalls his own search for the perfect golf swing, which he called "Excalibur." He confesses, ". . . we are always groping. We cannot grow as we should like because we have no roots. We are the earth's most changeable disciples, ever ready to try some new tap in the hope it will prove our salvation, equally ready to desert it for another if it does not give us what we want."

In golf there seem to be as many self-appointed teachers as there are players. While most players are searching for their "Excalibur," often they talk as if they have found the remedy to their golf swing and to everyone else's. Wise players will seek a capable pro to teach and guide them in achieving their potential.

While every individual walks a different path in life, we each have the opportunity for eternal life through faith in Jesus Christ. He is available to teach, guide, and instruct us through the eternal wisdom of the Bible. As in golf and life, this journey is not based on how much you have read, nor your level of knowledge. Instead, it is about your application of God's truth on the course of daily living.

We draw wisdom from the Bible, the original source of truth and inspiration, and from great golf players and teachers. Many of these writings about golf are nearly a century old. Like the Bible, they are as relevant today as when they were written. The parallels between the wisdom of the Bible and of great golfers over the past century are a rich source of inspiration for "playing the game." We too are playing the games of life and golf, and we are learning and growing with you.

THE *Greatest* GAME

Golf is deceptively simple and
endlessly complicated.
A child can play it well, and a grown
man can never master it.

Any single round of it is full of
unexpected triumphs
and seemingly perfect shots
that end in disaster.

It is almost a science, yet it is a puzzle
without an answer.
It is gratifying and tantalizing,
precise and unpredictable.

It requires complete concentration
and total relaxation.
It satisfies the soul and frustrates
the intellect.

It is at the same time rewarding
and maddening—and it is,
without a doubt, the greatest game
mankind has ever invented.

ANONYMOUS

Billy Graham

I never pray on a golf course.

Actually, the Lord answers

my prayers everywhere

except on the course.

INTRODUCTION

olf is clearly one of the most challenging and, at the same time, humbling experiences man has ever invented. Those of us who have been struck by the lure of the game can attest to its pleasures and frustrations. It has been called "the game of games" and "the noblest of all games." David Forgan wrote, "Golf is a science, the study of a lifetime, in which you can exhaust yourself but never your subject." Admittedly, at times it has also been called a few things that are far less endearing. Westbrook Pegler, a sportswriter, called golf "the most useless outdoor game ever devised to waste the time and try the spirit of man."

One of the attractions of golf is its many parallels to "the game of life." Life is also played on a course, the course of our life. As in golf, our daily walk through life brings new opportunities and new challenges. There is adversity to be avoided or overcome, the beauty of life and nature to be explored, and relationships with people and God to be developed.

The holes of many great golf courses, especially the old and famous ones, were named for an important feature of the hole. Examples include The Road Hole at St. Andrews and Troone's Postage Stamp with its small green. Sometimes the name reflects the skills needed, or the challenge faced by each player on that hole. Sections of golf courses have also been given names. The most famous example is the section of Augusta National called Amen Corner. Members, or pros playing in the Master's Tournament, may need to pray when they come to that difficult section of the course.

Playing the Game is about the parallels between the game of golf and the game of life. Those parallels are presented through an 18-hole course called The Rock because in both life and golf we need a solid foundation. Just as the grip is the foundation for the golf swing, Jesus is the foundation for our life—"a foundation upon the rock" (Luke 6:48).

The Rock has four sections: Understanding the Game, Preparing for the Game, Playing the Game, and Achieving Your Potential in the Game. Each hole on this inspirational golf course has a theme that is important for building a solid foundation for your life and golf. The name of the hole reflects the theme to be discovered in "playing" that hole. You will "play" each of the 18 holes by reading, reflecting on, and applying the wisdom and inspiration for the hole. Our goal is to help you gain competence in your quest to achieve your potential on whatever hole you find yourself, in life or golf. We want you to play with confidence, enjoying the thrill of each great shot planned and executed. We also want to encourage you in the frustrating and, at times, almost overwhelming challenges faced in life and in golf.

Whether you are practicing, playing alone or with friends, or competing on a team, we want to help you enjoy yourself and find fulfillment. Bobby Jones said, "The real way to enjoy playing golf is to take pleasure not in the score, but in the execution of the strokes." How true that is for life as well. We need to learn to take time to enjoy life. Ultimately, "the game" is about relationships with others and with Jesus. Jesus seeks to be your teacher, counselor, friend, and Savior. He is the ultimate pro, the only pro who can provide eternal wisdom and inspiration for your life. He is the only one who can really guide your way through the course of life. Live for, and enjoy, this important relationship with God.

In life, as in golf, we will never reach perfection, but we can continue to make progress. We hope you never grow tired of learning from the challenges and opportunities you will face on the course we have laid out for you. The holes are based upon those at The Players Club at Sawgrass in Ponte Verde Beach, Florida, one of the most beautiful courses in the world. Each year it is the site of The Player's Championship on the PGA Tour. Like any round of golf, we believe you will want to share with others your experiences and insights from playing The Rock. In conversations and in small groups you can explore these lessons for life and golf.

Have a great round! We hope The Rock helps you build a solid foundation for life and golf. We think you will find it to be a character-building experience.

THE *Enduring* LURE

There is no
royal road to success.

The path is not an easy one,—
which is one of the chief reasons
why golf has such an
enduring lure.

WALTER J. TRAVIS

Purpose

THE *Ultimate* AIM

Have a clear
vision of the target
and focus on it.
Have a well-defined
purpose for existence,
a reason for being and
an ultimate goal in life.

BOBBY CLAMPETT

Hebrews 12:1–2

Therefore, since we have so great a cloud of witnesses surrounding us, let us also lay aside every encumbrance, and the sin which so easily entangles us, and let us run with endurance the race that is set before us, fixing our eyes on Jesus, the author and perfecter of faith, who for the joy set before Him endured the cross, despising the shame, and has sat down at the right hand of the throne of God.

Needle's Eye

PAR 4 · 364 Yards

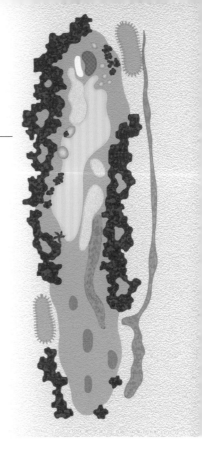

In playing this first hole, as in everything we do in life and golf, we must have a clear purpose and precise aim. It is a challenging par four that demands a tee shot so precise it could fly through the eye of a needle to a very narrow landing area. It's not enough to thread the needle; there is still the matter of the difficult approach to a tiny, elevated green guarded with bunkers. This hole is not very long, but to escape with par you must have your mind focused with purpose and execute precise shots.

Matthew 19:24

And again I say to you, it is easier for a camel to go through the eye of a needle, than for a rich man to enter the kingdom of God.

AIM *at* IT!

Define the target.

What is my

ultimate purpose?

Aim at it.

Set specific goals.

Visualize it.

BOBBY CLAMPETT

1 Timothy 6:11

But flee from

these things,

you man of God;

and pursue righteousness,

godliness, faith,

love, perseverance

and gentleness.

HARVEY PENICK

SINGLENESS *of* PURPOSE

Singleness of purpose!

That must be our attitude

towards every stroke we play.

True, it cannot be acquired

as easily as a new driver,

but acquired it can be,

even in a small degree,

if a player hopes to make

any real progress

in the game.

LESLIE SCHON

Isaiah 40:31

Yet those who

wait for the LORD

will gain new strength;

they will mount up

with wings like eagles,

they will run and

not get tired,

they will walk and

not become weary.

You belong to the power
you choose to obey.
My purpose in life
is to know God at any cost,
to pursue Him.

Obedience
apart from a relationship
ends in futility.

WALLY ARMSTRONG

WHERE *Is Your* FOCUS?

I am certain that there can be no freedom, and no natural swing in hitting the golf ball, if the mind is occupied by instructing the body.

J. H. TAYLOR
Renowned Golf Teacher of the 1920s

In 26 years of teaching golf, I find that the most common problem that destroys a golfer's play on the course is focusing on too many things.

WALLY ARMSTRONG

Psalm 37:4–5

Delight yourself

in the LORD;

and He will

give you the desires

of your heart.

Commit your way

to the LORD,

trust also in Him,

and He will do it.

Principles

LIKE *a* TREE

The fundamental
principles of golf
break down into:
Control, Balance,
and Timing.
All other things are
merely incidentals.

ERNEST JONES

Jeremiah 17:7–8

Blessed is the man

who trusts

in the LORD

and whose trust

is the LORD.

For he will be like

a tree planted

by the water,

that extends

its roots by

a stream. . . .

CONTROL
Balance
Timing

Giant Oaks

PAR 5 • 511 Yards

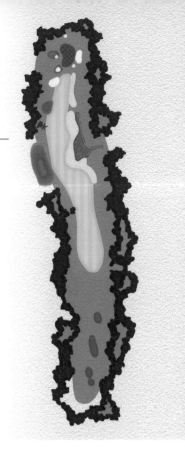

Large oak trees give this par five its beauty. The oaks are a symbol of wisdom, their limbs directing the player toward the fairway. Water runs the length of the right side of the hole. The second shot is best played to a ridge on the left side of the fairway to set up a good approach to the small green. If you stick to the principles of your swing and play the hole wisely, you'll do just fine.

Colossians 2:6–7

As you therefore have received Christ Jesus the Lord, so walk in Him, having been firmly rooted and now being built up in Him and established in your faith, just as you were instructed. . . .

THE *Golf* SWING

I've always believed the fundamentals

of the golf swing

are in a sense immutable,

that all good players

down through the

generations have achieved

certain goals demanded

by the laws of physics,

even though their styles

of doing so or their points

of emphasis may have varied.

JACK NICKLAUS

Psalm 1:1–2

How blessed is the man

who does not walk

in the counsel

of the wicked . . .

but his delight

is in the law

of the LORD,

and in His law

he meditates

day and night.

Gripping the golf club properly
is the key to
playing golf effectively.
Gripping God's Word fully
is the key to
living life effectively.

JIM SHEARD

SEE *the Whole* PICTURE

So far as the golf swing is concerned, in order to keep any part of it in perspective we must review the action as a whole. For it is at its best an unbroken motion. To stress one part unduly must destroy the rhythmic flow.

E. M. PRAIN

Even when working on only a certain part of the swing, always see it as part of the whole, starting with the pre-shot routine right on through to the flight of the ball, the spin on it and how it will bounce once it lands.

TOM LEHMAN
in *Live Hands*

The golfer, if he is to play well, must see his swing as a whole, both before he makes it and while he is making it.

ABE MITCHELL

John 1:1–4 paraphrased

Jesus is the whole picture in life.

FUNDAMENTALS
for Uncompromised
TIME WITH GOD

Set a spot—a definite time and place where your Bible, notebook and prayer lists are waiting for you.

Clear your mind—"Cease striving and know that I am God" (Psalm 46:10). Resist interruptions and distractions, guarding the intimacy of the time by concentrating on the person (God) you are with.

Open your hands—"Cuddle time" is time to turn all your concerns, schedule, questions, thanks, worry, over to God.

Get an assignment—A word for you from God through the Bible. It is not meeting with a book, but with God. We are looking for something to do, not just something to know. Apply God's words to what you are facing today.

Set your course—Think through the events and people that will be filling your day. Pray for each of them and turn them over to Christ. As you do, be attentive to any instructions or ideas He plants in your heart.

[When you step onto the tee of your life,] you will enjoy stability only to the degree that [your life is] rooted in a daily relationship with Christ.

RON HUTCHCRAFN
Peaceful Living in a Stressful World

Priorities

SUCCESS *Versus* SIGNIFICANCE

Success is measured by our accomplishments in life. In golf it is our score, our victories, and our handicap. In life it is our titles, our paycheck, and the things we acquire.

Significance is eternal.
It is reflected in our relationships with people and with Jesus.
It is revealed by commitment, trust, and where we spend our time.

JIM SHEARD

> **Matthew 6:33–34**
>
> *But seek first His kingdom and His righteousness; and all these things shall be added to you. Therefore do not be anxious for tomorrow; for tomorrow will care for itself. Each day has enough trouble of its own.*

Dead End

PAR 3 • 139 Yards

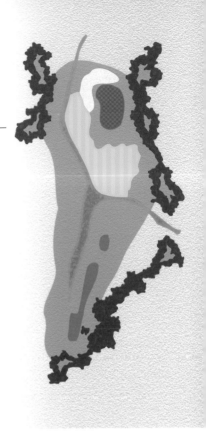

This par three is very short but has plenty of trouble if you go for the pin and miss the green. That could lead to a dead end early in the round by costing you a stroke or two. So, don't be greedy and seek short-term success. Instead, the way to play this hole is to aim for the center of the green, regardless of the pin location. By hitting this green in regulation you are on your way to a birdie, or an easy par. Play the percentage shot, take your par or birdie, and move on to number four. That can be quite significant this early in the game.

Proverbs 16:25

There is a way which seems right to a man, but its end is the way of death.

PLEASURE *in* EXECUTION

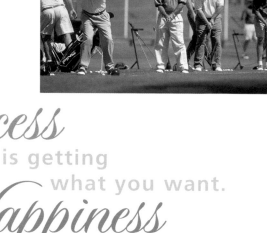

Success is getting what you want.
Happiness is wanting what you get.

ANONYMOUS

The real way to enjoy playing golf is to take pleasure not in the score, but in the execution of the strokes.

BOBBY JONES

1 Thessalonians 5:18

In everything

give thanks;

for this is

God's will for you

in Christ Jesus.

SLAVES *to* *the* SCORECARD

The continual striving to improve our score, although entirely natural, nevertheless does detract to some extent from our ability to enjoy golf. When we become slaves to the card and pencil, we become inclined to regard as total losses those rounds in which our score mounts beyond our reasonable expectancy.

When we take pleasure in the game only according to the scorecard, a bad start is likely to put entirely away the possibility of an enjoyable afternoon.

BOBBY JONES

I guess the best way to avoid getting uptight is to be realistic about yourself.

- Realize you're going to hit some shots well . . . and some badly.

- You'll win some matches . . . and lose some.

- It really isn't the end of the world . . . either way.

Even the professionals who make their living at the game have to think this way.

It is, especially for you, just a game.

BYRON NELSON

God wants us to take our *thoughts* and *plans* to Him. In fact, *He* wants us to *seek Him first* in all things.

(See Matthew 6:33)

MAXIMIZE *Your* GAME: FOCUS *on* SIGNIFICANCE

1. *Stand firm in the Lord* (Philippians 4:1). God won't let you down, let go of you, or give up on you.

2. *Be mission-minded* (Philippians 4:14). Paul planted churches with the Philippians' support.

3. *Be open-hearted* (Philippians 4:15–16). The Philippians sent Paul aid again and again.

4. *See giving as an investment* (Philippians 4:17), not a sacrifice. Give up small ambitions and put your resources at God's disposal.

5. *Care about what God thinks* (Philippians 4:18). Make an offering pleasing to Him. Want what God wants in spite of what you want.

6. *Trust God to provide* (Philippians 4:19). God will meet your needs.

7. *Let God have His way* (Philippians 4:6). God will complete the work.

8. *Pray* (Philippians 4:19). Take your needs to the Lord in prayer.

9. *Live consistently* (Philippians 4:29–30). Suffer for Jesus Christ as Paul did.

STEVEN ANDERSON, SENIOR PASTOR,
BETHEL CHURCH, OWATONNA, MN

The Swing

A *Solid* FOUNDATION

Standing properly to the ball is just as vital in assuring an easy swinging action as is the proper placing of the hands. Where your feet are placed determines the ease with which the body responds during the action of the swing. Their position—in relation to each other and to where the ball rests—fixes the foundation for the action of the stroke.

ERNEST JONES

1 Corinthians 15:58

Be steadfast,
immovable,
always abounding
in the work
of the Lord,
knowing that
your toil is
not in vain
in the Lord.

Position

The Master's Touch

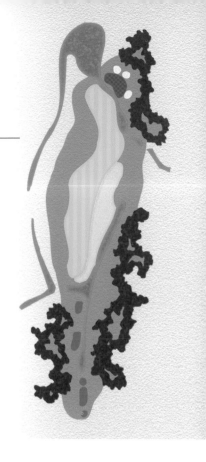

This challenging par four reveals the Master's touch in its design and beauty. Only the combined skills of the Master designer of nature and the course designer could create such beauty. The golf swing is also a thing of beauty when the parts work together in one complete circle of power and grace. In addition to the need for a solid foundation, there can be no weak link in your swing or it will be revealed under the testing of this work of God and man. Any flaws in your swing will be revealed by the difficulty of the tee shot and the requirement for another solid shot to reach the bulk-headed green.

1 Corinthians 3:10–11

As a wise master builder
I laid a foundation, and
another is building upon it.
But let each man be careful
how he builds upon it. For no
man can lay a foundation
other than the one which is laid,
which is Jesus Christ.

33 • The Swing: A *Solid* Foundation

THE *Golf* SWING

I had puzzled over the correct golf swing,

wondering if there was such a thing.

It seemed to me that there must be some trick

about it. How is it that little fellows hit long shots

and big fellows sometimes get nowhere.

Certainly there was a secret carefully

guarded by those who mastered it. . . .

There might be no road to proficiency,

but then again there might.

ALFRED PADGHAM

CONFIDENCE *in the* CIRCLE

For me confidence in the swing is built upon . . . the feeling of the circle as it is revolving around the spine with the hands forming the inner circle and the clubhead forming the outer circle.

Implementation involves . . . setting the circle to the ground, aiming the circle, supporting the circle, empowering the circle, and finally trusting the circle.

WALLY ARMSTRONG

God is in charge of the earth.
He is the creator.
He empowers it.

Isaiah 40:22

It is He who sits above

the vault of the earth. . . .

A Composition

It will be found that the sound swing is *very graceful.*

BOBBY JONES

The correct hitting motion

is one unbroken thrust

from the beginning of the downswing

to the end of the follow-through.

BEN HOGAN

If to this we add

a sense of balance,

a sense of unhurried calm,

a feeling that there is lots of time

to feel each movement blending into the

others, we shall begin to feel the true golf rhythm.

PERCY BOOMER

The *golf swing* is a composition, not a medley

KEN VENTURI

Planning

SURVEY *the* LAND

Walter Hagan surveyed the land to determine how he would play the course. Ben Hogan planned every shot for the round and then played them over and over in his mind. They had a plan for the course. We need a course strategy for life that guides the achievement of our ultimate purpose.

> **Proverbs 22:17**
>
> *Incline your ear and hear the words of the wise, and apply your mind to my knowledge. . . .*

Quicksand

PAR 4 · 408 Yards

This par four is very long and has fairway bunkers all the way down the right side. Play your tee shot safely to the left side of the fairway or it could be like a day at the beach. The green is guarded in front by a large dip and sand bunkers that are so deceptively hidden they become like quicksand to the player. So, survey the land, make your plan, and don't try to cut corners. Step up to the tee with a clear commitment to your plan for playing the hole and each shot.

Proverbs 16:9

The mind of man plans his way, but the LORD directs his steps.

MAKING a PLAN

Making a plan is what separates great players from good players. Hogan, Snead, Nelson, Palmer, Nicklaus, Trevino, Watson . . . the list goes on, they all had complete mastery of the mental side of golf.

TOM LEHMAN
in *Live Hands*

Proverbs 19:21

Many are the plans
in a man's heart,
but the counsel
of the LORD,
it will stand.

A plan of attack must be sound, based on solid, well-tested principles. . . . We must think hard and constructively, and then we must act quickly while the plan is fresh in mind. It is fatal to change the plan half-way through the operation.

ERIC PRAIN

USING YOUR *head*
is what course
STRATEGY
is all about.

— BYRON NELSON

RIGHT *Choices*

Course management is making the right choices. To do that you need to analyze the situation.

<small>Scott Simpson</small>

Sometimes it is not how hard we try, but what we choose to try.

SUCCESSFUL *Course* STRATEGY

Having a course strategy and controlling your mind on the golf course is necessary if you're going to be a successful player. . . . That involves knowing where to hit the ball, what kind of shot to play under different circumstances and which club you must select to pull it off. [You need] the right mental plan so that you can first make the proper shot-making decisions, then execute them with a good swing.

Be Realistic, about your inherent capabilities, and how well you are playing to those on any given day.

Play Within Yourself. Establish a realistic style of play and don't try to exceed your limitations. Avoid hitting each shot so hard that your swing goes out of control. Make each swing with something less than an all-out effort.

Don't Even Think About Mechanics.
Realistically, you might even have two swing thoughts—a backswing thought and a downswing thought, perhaps. These thoughts should be programmed as much as possible into your subconscious before you swing. . . .

Play Decisively. Once you choose how to play a shot and what club to use, don't change that decision unless some unusual circumstance forces you to.

Be Aggressive. Don't play defensively or hesitantly. Think that you're going to hit each shot well instead of trying not to hit it badly. Don't be looking for trouble. Look instead for a successful shot.

BYRON NELSON
"Shape Your Swing the Modern Way"

Practice

NO *Royal* ROAD

You learn to swing only through practice. There is no royal road to skill, whether it is golf or any other sport, occupation, or avocation.

ERNEST JONES

> Proverbs 15:19
>
> *The way of the sluggard is as a hedge of thorns, but the path of the upright is a highway.*

Knowing I've practiced effectively to strengthen my game gives me added confidence on the course.

TOM LEHMAN

Narrow Gates

PAR 4 · 351 Yards

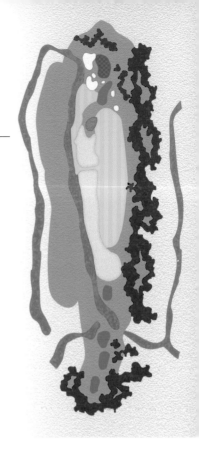

You have to rely on previous practice to be able to negotiate through the two narrow gates on this interesting par four. Destruction awaits those who miss their shot on either gate. First, you have to place your tee shot just short of the narrow neck in the fairway. If you hit too long or wide, you will have failed to make it through the first gate. Then your challenge is to hit an approach through a very narrow gate formed by pot bunkers and palms in front of the green. You can only learn to accomplish this feat through lots of practice. There is no royal road.

Matthew 7:13–14

Enter by the narrow gate; for the gate is wide, and the way is broad that leads to destruction, and many are those who enter by it. For the gate is small, and the way is narrow that leads to life, and few are those who find it.

PRACTICE *to Improve*

All golfers,

men and women, professional and amateur,

are united by one thing: their desire to improve.

JUDY RANKIN
FORMER LPGA PRO AND GOLF ANNOUNCER

We gain in life and golf

the old-fashioned way:

we earn it through

hard work and practice.

There are
**no shortcuts
to SUCCESS;**
it takes time.

PRACTICE

Practice is the major key to improvement.

Lay out a practice plan to prepare yourself.

Practice as you play. Play as you practice.

Play imaginary holes on the practice range.

Practice difficult shots prior to going out onto the course.

Practice all parts of your game.

Rely on good instruction, coaching, and training aids.

PRACTICE *New* IDEAS

Try out new ideas in practice—not in actual play. Never make a violent change in methods.

Don't attempt to immediately put tips into your game.

The change in the mechanics of golfing requires *patience* and *practice.* These are the two greatest words in golf.

Each change,

if soundly arrived at,

can thus be made to

yield golfing dividends

in progress and greater skill.

CHESTER HORTON
"Better Golf"

Proverbs 13:4

The soul of the sluggard

craves and gets nothing,

but the soul of the diligent

is made fat.

DISCIPLINED *Muscles*

To play par golf it not only is necessary to get all your muscles properly trained, but it is essential to keep them disciplined, since they won't long stay trained otherwise.

Two or three easy practice swings provide the right disciplining. They provide a sort of rehearsal of good company manners.

Chester Horton

Hebrews 12:6–7

For those whom the Lord loves He disciplines, and He scourges every son whom He receives. It is for discipline that you endure; God deals with you as sons; for what son is there whom his father does not discipline?

Preparation

MASTER *an* IDEAL

By repeating what
the pupil must learn,
I have taught hundreds
of people to play golf . . .
although in the final analysis
it is really they who have
taught themselves to master
an ideal which I set before them.

ERNEST JONES

> **Isaiah 30:20–21**
>
> *Your eyes will*
>
> *behold your Teacher.*
>
> *And your ears will*
>
> *hear a word behind you,*
>
> *"This is the way, walk in it,"*
>
> *whenever you turn*
>
> *to the right or to the left.*

God teaches us in a similar manner.
He shows us the ideal way that He
has set before us.

Carpenter's Workbench

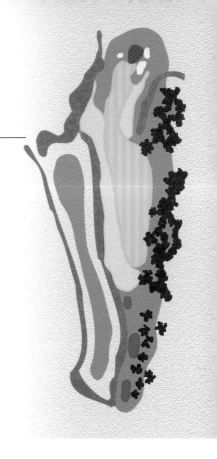

This difficult par four was carefully laid out on the designer's workbench. You are being prepared for challenges like this by your teacher and your own preparation. The tee shot is to a wide fairway. That still leaves a long second shot to a green that is surrounded by bunkers and a pond. If your tee shot is not long enough, follow the advice of most teachers and be willing to lay up on your second shot. Then rely on the ideal model for the short game that you have learned from your teacher.

Isaiah 44:13

[A carpenter] shapes wood,

he extends a measuring line;

he outlines it with red chalk.

He works it with planes,

and outlines it with a compass,

and makes it like the form of

a man, like the beauty of man,

so that it may sit in a house.

INSTRUCTION *from a* PRO

Only 8 percent of the golfers in America take lessons. That means 92 percent choose not to take lessons.

This accounts for all those who take up the game, play badly, and then quit in frustration.

So many more could enjoy the game and become proficient at playing if they would invest the time and money in lessons from a competent instructor. This is the only wise way to obtain the knowledge and skills needed to progress.

Proverbs 1:7

The fear of the LORD is the beginning of knowledge; fools despise wisdom and instruction.

THE *Setup*

If you set up correctly there is a
chance you'll hit a reasonable shot,
even if you make a mediocre swing. . . .
If you set up incorrectly, you'll hit
a lousy shot even if you make
the greatest swing in the world.

JACK NICKLAUS

We have the opportunity to set ourselves up
properly with God. We do this through faith and
by seeking after the principles found in God's Word.
In spite of our own imperfections and limitations,
when we do that, He can utilize us and bring forth
victory in our life.

PREPARING *for Action*

I've always believed
that success is achieved
when proper preparation
meets opportunity.

Tom Lehman
in *Live Hands*

You win by working—

by concentration

and desire. . . .

The key is preparation.

You have to be prepared.

Patty Berg

Proverbs 21:30–31

There is no wisdom

and no understanding

and no counsel

against the Lord.

The horse is prepared

for the day of battle,

but victory belongs

to the Lord.

Time
with God
is the preparation for
each day of your life.

Jim Sheard

Progress

Unattainable PERFECTION

The game of golf is a game
of accepting imperfection;
of realizing that the perfect
game has never been played,
never will be played,
or ever could be played.

ANONYMOUS

Only one person has
been perfect, and He was
the Son of God.

Hebrews 5:8–9

Although He was a Son,

He learned obedience

from the things

which He suffered.

And having been

made perfect,

He became to all those

who obey Him

the source of

eternal salvation. . . .

Son of God

Chapel in the Pines

PAR 3 · 201 Yards

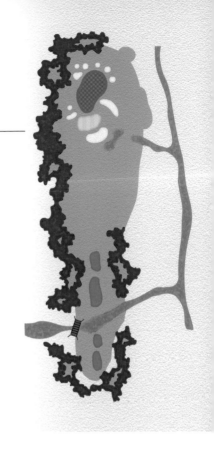

This beautiful golf hole is reminiscent of the magnificence of Augusta National, which Thomas Boswell has called "18 chapels carved out of the pines." Carved out of the beauty of nature, it reminds us that only God can create perfection. It is a long par three with a huge green. Take plenty of club for your tee shot. However, because of the large green, your shot does not have to be perfect for you to be putting. Just take the club you select and let it fly. If you must strive for perfection, let it be on the putt that will await you at the green.

Psalm 50:1–2

The Mighty One, God,
the LORD, has spoken,
and summoned the earth
from the rising of the sun
to its setting. Out of Zion,
the perfection of beauty,
God has shown forth.

NEAR *Perfection*?

We never come anywhere near perfection— there is always something *left to improve.*

BEN HOGAN

The Bible speaks of how all have sinned and fall short of the glory of God. Life, like golf, is a game of misses and imperfection.

In life, as in golf, we must not base our significance on being perfect. God does not expect us to be sinless, just to sin less. That is called progress.

It is a process of learning to trust Him to take hold of our hand, imperfections, possessions, and life.

Golf is not a game of *GREAT SHOTS.*

IT'S A *game* OF
the most accurate *misses.*
THE PEOPLE who *win*
make the *smallest mistakes.*

GENE LITTLER

THE *Perfect* GOLFER

I have pictured the average golfer as a man of many vices and few virtues; I have suggested that he modify his temperament, instead of allowing the game to modify it for him; that he sublimate his passions; and that if he cannot control himself he cannot expect to control his club; I have scoffed at his superstitions; and made a mockery of the good resolutions that he makes, and breaks.

All this, when I know quite well that if, by a freak of Nature, there ever arose a Perfect Golfer, he would have to give up the game because no one would play with him.

Neither you nor I would care to play with a superman who never made a mistake.

But surely it is better to chase the will-o'-the-wisp of unattainable perfection than to strive after a lesser ideal.

LESLIE SCHON
The Psychology of Golf

ACCEPT *Imperfection*

olf is a game made up of errors. Learning to cope with feelings of failure and imperfections is one of the keys to freeing the mind and allowing oneself to play to the best of one's physical ability. . . . Free the mind of the fear of failure and the game can be played in an uninhibited, fully productive way. Mastery of the art of playing golf well undoubtedly rests upon mastery of the art of playing poorly.

Only by learning to accept imperfection and to play without fear can one perfect both the golf swing and the art of scoring.

VIVIEN SAUNDERS
The Golfing Mind

2 Timothy 1:7

For God has not given us
a spirit of timidity,
but of power and love
and discipline.

People

Lasting IMPRESSIONS

If your life doesn't demand a supernatural explanation, you haven't earned the right to be heard.

STEPHEN OLFORD

2 Corinthians 5:20

Therefore, we are ambassadors for Christ, as though God were entreating through us; we beg you on behalf of Christ, be reconciled to God.

The Ambassador

PAR 5 · 554 Yards

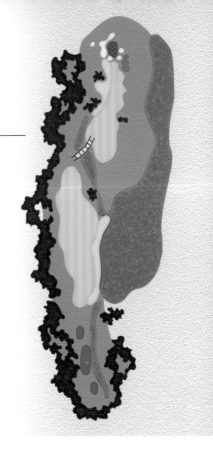

This hole is an ambassador for the whole course. It incorporates the need for length off the tee, accuracy for the second shot, and short game prowess to play the tiny crowned green. This magnificent opportunity must be enjoyed with others. To play this hole, and the course, alone, would be to miss the delight in sharing the experience with others. You too can be an ambassador for God and golf as you play the game. Encourage fellow players and be a good example so that you are salt and light to one another.

Matthew 5:16

Let your light
shine before men
in such a way that
they may see your
good works, and
glorify your Father
who is in heaven.

BE A BLESSING *to Others*

Finally, remember that the game is designed for your pleasure. Therefore cultivate the habit of fair thinking about the rubs of fortune; learn to recognize your good luck and offset it against the bad. You will enjoy your game that way, as a man should, and you will give your partner a better chance to enjoy his.

ABE MITCHELL

Luke 6:31

And just as you want people to treat you, treat them in the same way.

Proverbs 22:1

A good name is to be more desired than great riches, favor is better than silver and gold.

The golf course, like the rest of life, is a place where we need to be a blessing, not a burden, to those around us.

JIM SHEARD

SHOW *You* CARE

Before people care
what you know, they have to know
that you care.

1 Peter 3:8

To sum up,

let all be

harmonious,

sympathetic,

brotherly,

kindhearted,

and humble

in spirit. . . .

Your Life IS JESUS TO Someone

Your life is Jesus to someone,
though tattered and torn it may be.
Though often times weak and unstable,
you're all of God someone will see.

Your tongue is Jesus to someone.
That idle, insensitive word
reflects to at least one searching heart
an idle, insensitive Lord.

Your goals are Jesus to someone.
What you put first they believe
are the goals of God for the Christian.
Your life is all they receive.

Your faithfulness—that's Jesus to someone.
Their judgment of how God is true
rests unquestionably in the faithfulness
they see day by day in you.

Your love is Jesus to someone—

that someone who is seeking to know

that Jesus will follow and guide and

befriend wherever in life they might go.

So beware lest others blaspheme

God by what you say or do,

for the only Jesus that someone knows

is the Jesus they see in you.

RUSSELL KELFER

Play Each Shot

See IT, Feel IT, Trust IT

Psalm 119:15

Visualize your shot first. Then trust the images you see, trust the mechanics that you've practiced, and simply be a shot maker.

WALLY ARMSTRONG

I will meditate on Thy precepts, and regard Thy ways.

The Catapult

PAR 4 • 373 Yards

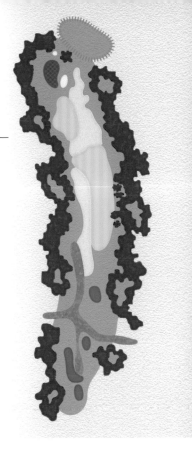

Trusting your swing is the key to playing this hole. Like a catapult, you must launch a high, soft shot from the tee onto the fairway. This requires visualizing your shot going to the point where the fairway doglegs left to the green. It is hard to go for the pin on your approach to this difficult green. To do so you will again need to catapult a high, soft shot to just the right location on the green. Do not let the hazards take your focus away from your swing. Instead, focus on the target and learn to use this sequence for every shot you play: See it, feel it, trust it.

Proverbs 22:19

So that your trust

may be in the LORD,

I have taught

you today,

even you.

SEE, *Feel*, TRUST

always emphasize this concept in teaching about performance in golf and in all of life. It helps golfers improve their performance as they learn to "see it, feel it, and trust it."

Golf professionals and amateurs, athletes, and people performing challenging tasks in their work need to SEE a clear picture of the target (what they want to have happen), to FEEL what it will be like to execute, and then to TRUST themselves to follow through to achieve that image.

I have taught collegiate and Olympic athletes, professional and amateur golfers, business professionals, and young people how to use these fundamental ideas to achieve their goals.

By learning to "see it, feel it, and trust it," they gain a "mental advantage" in golf and life.

This concept helps them convert their desire and ability to perform into actual successful performance.

DAVID L. COOK, PH.D.
SPORTS PSYCHOLOGIST

COURSE *Performance*

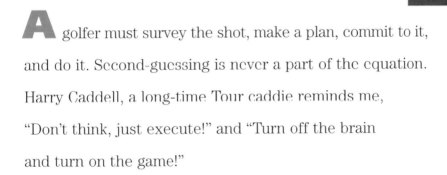

The body can't achieve what the mind can't conceive. The body can't produce what the mind can't induce. If you can't see it in your mind, don't expect your body to perform it on the course.

WALLY ARMSTRONG

A golfer must survey the shot, make a plan, commit to it, and do it. Second-guessing is never a part of the equation. Harry Caddell, a long-time Tour caddie reminds me, "Don't think, just execute!" and "Turn off the brain and turn on the game!"

What he's saying is don't get in your own way by over-analyzing everything. Be more like a fearless kid, and like the Nike slogan says, "Just do it!"

TOM LEHMAN
in *Live Hands*

> ### Proverbs 16:3
>
> *Commit your works to the LORD, and your plans will be established.*

poetry

What OTHER PEOPLE may find in poetry or *art museums*, I find in the *flight* of a GOOD DRIVE—the white ball *sailing* up into the BLUE SKY, growing *smaller* and *smaller*, then suddenly reaching its apex, *curving, falling* and finally DROPPING to the turf to roll some more, *just* the way I PLANNED IT.

ARNOLD PALMER

Strengths

INSIDE *Every* PERSON

As I teach the golf swing to my students, my passion is to draw out a perfect swing from their dysfunctional efforts to hit the ball. Inside every person there's a golf swing that's based upon sound golf and physical principles such as centrifugal force and leverage. I want to help each person bring harmony from chaos; to allow their swing to flow out from within.

WALLY ARMSTRONG

> ### 1 Samuel 16:7
>
> *But the LORD said to Samuel, "Do not look at his appearance or at the height of his stature, because I have rejected him; for God sees not as man sees, for man looks at the outward appearance, but the LORD looks at the heart."*

Lion Heart

PAR 5 · 509 Yards

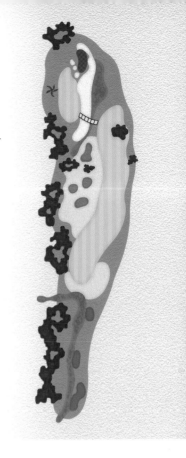

After your drive there are many ways to play this hole. You must choose the one best suited to your skills and strengths. You may risk a long second shot to the left over a stream and be left with a short pitch to the green. Or you can choose a safe, short shot to the right. However, on your approach shot from this angle you will need to carry the water in front of the green. For many players, a bogey here might be a good score, considering the full range of possibilities. Only those with a "lion heart" will have the courage to choose the best route for their ability and strengths.

John 7:37–38

Now on the last day, the great day of the feast, Jesus stood and cried out, saying, "If any man is thirsty, let him come to Me and drink. He who believes in Me, as the Scripture said, 'From his innermost being shall flow rivers of living water.' "

know your
game

I've always believed that golfers *need to know* their
own game, WHAT THEY'RE CAPABLE OF, and what
they're not. Know these things so *you can formulate*
a game plan and MAKE GOOD DECISIONS
for *each course* and *each round.*

Tom Lehman
in *Live Hands*

A TRINITY *of Games* IN ONE

Golf is really a trinity of games—three in one.

There is . . . the drive, the approach, and the putt.

In the long game, distance and a fair measure of accuracy are the cardinal requirements; . . . the approach calls for regulated strength, plus accuracy of direction, for all kinds of distances and from a variety of lies; . . . while the putt is a modified approach combining accuracy of the highest degree, joined to delicacy of touch.

Ability in any one of the three departments does not necessarily carry with skill in the other two. It is the coordination of all three at one and the same time that spells success.

WALTER J. TRAVIS
"Building Up a Game"

Acts 10:38

You know of Jesus of Nazareth, how God anointed Him with the Holy Spirit and with power. . . .

PLAY *Your* GAME

Have realistic expectations.

Take responsibility for your actions—don't blame someone or something.

Play the percentages based on your strengths and the demands of the course.

Evaluate your own scores and identify your strengths.

> **Romans 12:6**
>
> *And since we have gifts that differ according to the grace given to us, let each exercise them accordingly. . . .*

Precision Shots

STROKE *Savers*

Luke 16:10–11

For reasons too obvious to state, of all the shots in golf, the short shots are most telling. No one can become a good scratch golfer without an effective short game.

ERIC PRAIN

He who is faithful in a very little thing is faithful also in much; and he who is unrighteous in a very little thing is unrighteous also in much. If therefore you have not been faithful in the use of unrighteous mammon, who will entrust the true riches to you

The Treasury

The beauty of number 12 is in the opportunity to score with the stroke-saving short game. The green on this short par four is hidden by a large mound. This forces the player to visualize his approach. Should you find yourself in one of the nearby bunkers, skill in playing sand shots will be important. Many have saved par here with a good sand-save or a great chip. Remember, like the widow's two copper coins, the little shots pay big dividends and contribute much to the treasury of your golf scores. Your investment in practicing the wide array of precision golf shots will be rewarded on every hole.

Mark 12:42-43

A poor widow came and put in two small copper coins, which amount to a cent. And calling His disciples to Him, [Jesus] said to them, "Truly I say to you, this poor widow put in more than all the contributors. . . ."

ROUTE *to Lower* SCORES

The player who recognizes
that he needs to devote
his head and hands to
improving his short game
sees the right route
to lower scores.

TOMMY ARMOUR

One of the
first things a novice has to
learn is that the simplest
stroke in golf may be big
with fate.—But in truth,
in golf there is no such
thing as a simple stroke.

ARNOLD HAULTAIN

THE 60-60 *Principle*

There is a 60-60 principle. Sixty percent of the shots are taken from within 60 yards of the hole. Despite this fact, most people do not practice the short game. The discipline to practice the short game takes commitment.

All you have to do is watch the Tour players practice and you'll see how much time they practice around the greens. You'll realize the importance of this short-game practice. It is how they train their fingers and hands to function effectively in the short shots.

WALLY ARMSTRONG

Psalm 144:1

Blessed be the LORD, my rock,

Who trains my hands for war,

and my fingers for battle. . . .

short *shots*

The short shots are best regarded simply as *drives in miniature,* and the same principle holds. GRIP LIGHTLY; stand *naturally*; avoid *tension;* FEEL the clubhead in the hands, and *MINDFUL ALWAYS* of its *purpose*, swing it with them crisply *through the ball.*

E. M. PRAIN

Putting

Fearless FINESSE

If you look upon putting with fear and trembling, well, the pixies that dance about the greens will turn your ball to one side or another when it is going straight for the hole.

ANDRA KIRKALDY

> **Proverbs 2:2–5**
>
> *Make your ear attentive to wisdom, incline your heart to understanding; for if you cry for discernment, lift your voice for understanding; if you seek her as silver, and search for her as for hidden treasures; then you will discern the fear of the LORD, and discover the knowledge of God.*

Toil or Pleasure

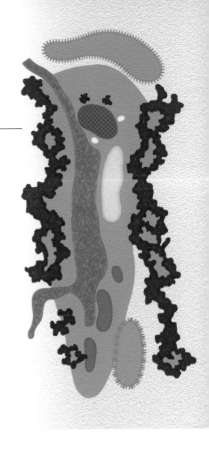

This hole is about putting. This short par three, like many holes on the course, is won or lost with the putter in hand. Here you are faced with an incredible two-tiered green. You have the choice of making it a toil or a pleasure. To make it a pleasure you must overcome your fears of putting, take a proper stance, become confident through practice, and learn to read the speed and direction of greens. Make the putter your ally and it will be a pleasure for you to use and a powerful weapon in your bag.

Psalm 16:11

Thou wilt make known to me the path of life; in Thy presence is fulness of joy; in Thy right hand there are pleasures forever.

PUTTING *is not* SIMPLE

Compared to the rest of golf, putting looks easy.
The ball always rests atop a manicured surface, inviting
solid contact. There are no trees, bunkers, water hazards
or out-of-bounds areas to heighten the challenge.
The putting stroke itself is relatively short and elementary.

Then why does putting create so much frustration,
even consternation? . . . And why do otherwise logical
men and women, who dedicate so many hours each week
to the sport, seldom, if ever, practice the part that uses
up some 30 to 50 percent of their shots? . . .

Putting is *not* that simple.

It demands constant attention—practice.

PAUL RUNYAN
The Short Way to Lower Scoring

A *Four-Foot* PUTT

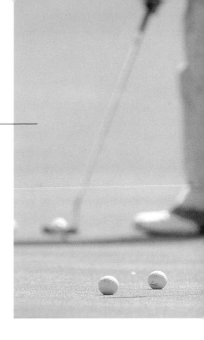

shot a wild elephant in Africa 30 yards from me, and it didn't hit the ground until it was right at my feet. I wasn't a bit scared, but a four-foot putt scares me to death.

SAM SNEAD

A good putt is speedily forgotten, *a bad putt* lingers in the memory.

LESLIE SCHON

Philippians 3:13–14

Brethren, I do not regard myself as having laid hold of it yet; but one thing I do: forgetting what lies behind and reaching forward to what lies ahead, I press on toward the goal for the prize of the upward call of God in Christ Jesus.

THE *Essence of* PUTTING

Unless he can see clearly in his mind's eye the whole journey of the ball from start to finish, he cannot shape the shot as a whole and so he will not make a rhythmic swing. If there is no rhythm the stroke is a mis-hit whatever the result may be. Rhythm is the essence of good putting.

ABE MITCHELL

Confidence has to be the golfer's greatest single weapon on the greens. . . . [This requires:]

the ability to read greens: to be able to judge very accurately where and at what speed the ball must roll to reach the hole. . . .

the ability to aim the ball where you've decided it should go.

the ability to repeatedly stroke the ball in a way that transmits a feeling of fluid, yet solid, contact from the clubface to the hands.

JACK NICKLAUS

Putting is a fine art. It requires the most delicate and *educated* touch.

ARNOLD HAULTAIN

Power Shots

EFFORTLESS *Power*

A swing is the most powerful action that it is possible to create, and is, at the same time, as close to effortless power as it is possible to get.

ERNEST JONES

1 Corinthians 2:3–5

And I was with you in weakness and in fear and in much trembling. And my message and my preaching were not in persuasive words of wisdom, but in demonstration of the Spirit and of power, that your faith should not rest on the wisdom of men, but on the power of God.

Giant's Glare

PAR 4 · 418 Yards

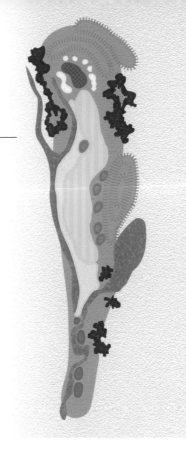

This is the most intimidating of the par fours. From the tee box you face a long runway with no sight of the green. The second shot is to a green nestled in the valley below. You might feel like David facing the glare of the mighty giant, Goliath. But you have the same opportunity that young David had. Don't be intimidated, and don't try to swing too hard. Instead, have faith and confidence. With the power of centrifugal force and the circle of the swing, you have the tools to face this giant's glare head-on. You can have effortless power to face even the most difficult challenges.

1 Samuel 17:47–49

And David put his hand

into his bag and took from it

a stone and slung it,

and struck the Philistine

on his forehead.

And the stone sank into

his forehead, so that he fell

on his face to the ground.

SOURCES *of power*

We gather up power through our physical make-up, but the gathering up and redirecting has to be guided by our sense of feel. The instant that sense of feel is lost or becomes disconnected our swing becomes disconnected also—and our power evaporates into thin air, like the sparkle from champagne when the cork is left out!

PERCY BOOMER

In our life it is the power of the Holy Spirit that has a powerful and lasting impact. Receiving and releasing this power requires submission to the three-part God— Father, Son, and Holy Spirit.

POWER *that Works*

With God's power at work in us we are able to do more than we could have imagined *on our own.*

Ephesians 3:20–21

Now to Him who is able

to do exceeding abundantly

beyond all that we ask

or think according to the

power that works within us,

to Him be the glory in the

church and in Christ Jesus

to all generations forever

and ever. Amen.

A *Tigerish* LASH

The fact is, business really begins with the golf stroke, when the club is about two thirds of the way to the ball on the downswing. It is then that the player must imitate the action of a tiger: stiffen the sinews, summon up the blood, and go right through with a swish.

J. H. TAYLOR

The Big Show is a performance in the fine art of hitting. . . . The action is that of whipping the clubhead through the ball with the hands. Not slapping it, waving it, slinging it, stiff-arming it, but whipping it with a tigerish lash. . . . The great hitters in golf are those who move their hands faster than those whose distance and precision are inferior.

TOMMY ARMOUR

2 Peter 1:3

His divine power has granted to us everything pertaining to life and godliness, through the true knowledge of Him who called us by His own glory and excellence.

Summing up,
**when a
golfer swings,
he produces
timed force.**

ERNEST JONES

Adversity

REJOICE *in* HOPE

Adversity is at
the very essence of
the game of golf.

JIM SHEARD

James 1:16–17

Do not be deceived,

my beloved brethren.

Every good thing bestowed

and every perfect gift is

from above, coming down

from the Father of lights,

with whom there is no

variation, or shifting shadow.

Romans 12:12

. . . rejoicing in hope,

persevering in tribulation,

devoted to prayer . . .

Valley of the Shadow

PAR 4 • 413 Yards

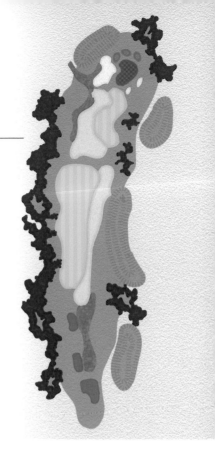

There are always shadows on this hole that create confusion and doubt in the player's mind. In addition, the tee shot is like hitting into a tunnel and across a watery valley. That valley must be crossed, and it spells destruction for those who fail to overcome their fear on this hole. This requires you to trust your tee shot. Once the adversity of this chasm has been traversed, the golfer finds green pastures and still waters. Once you are in the fairway you can comfortably approach the double-terraced green surrounded by tall pines. The difficult part of this hole is behind you.

Psalm 23:4

Even though I walk

through the valley

of the shadow of death,

I fear no evil;

for Thou art with me;

Thy rod and Thy staff,

they comfort me.

UP *in a* TREE

In a tournament in England in 1982, I was playing the 17th hole when I pulled my second shot, a nine iron, to the left. I heard the ball hit a big oak tree near the green two or three times, but never saw it come down. As I approached the green I could hear the spectators laughing. Sure enough, the ball was lodged up in the tree about 15 feet above the ground in a little indentation on a huge branch. I debated whether I should take the penalty shot or climb up in the tree and hit it. Remembering the Langers don't give up easily, I decided to climb up in the oak tree. Minutes later, I hit the ball from up in the trees and onto the green.

[Later, in the United States,] I heard a couple in the crowd talking about me. "There's the guy who was in the tree," one spectator said. "What's his name?" The other replied, "I think it's Bernhard something." "No it's not. That's Tarzan!"

BERNHARD LANGER
The LINKS Letter

THE *Bunkers* OF LIFE

It has often been said that bunkers are not placed on golf courses to catch bad shots, but to punish shots that are not quite good enough. The golfer, when he finds his ball deep in a bunker, should remember this sage remark, and draw much consolation from it.

LESLIE SCHON

Count it all joy"
when you hit into a bunker!
View it as a part of the process
of becoming a more steadfast and
complete golfer.

James 1:2–4

Consider it all joy, my brethren, when you encounter various trials, knowing that the testing of your faith produces endurance. And let endurance have its perfect result, that you may be perfect and complete, lacking in nothing.

Golf **is good for the character in many ways**

Arnold Haultain

Perseverance

STEADY *Endurance*

1 Peter 1:3–4, 6

I want the same discipline
in my faith that I have
in my golf game.

SCOTT SIMPSON

God wants you to
persevere with Him,
and He will help you
do just that.

*Blessed be the God and Father
of our Lord Jesus Christ,
who according to His
great mercy has caused us
to be born again to a living
hope through the resurrection
of Jesus Christ from the dead,
to obtain an inheritance. . . .
In this you greatly rejoice,
even though now for a little
while, if necessary,
you have been distressed
by various trials.*

The Furnace

PAR 5 · 491 Yards

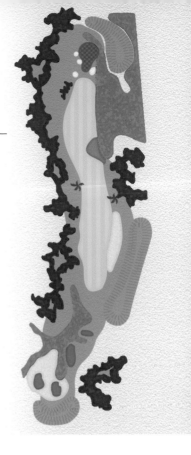

Three pressure shots could make this hole feel like a furnace of heat and fire. Therefore, the strategy here must be one of perseverance and patience. Play the hole the way it was designed with a good tee shot and a nicely placed lay-up short of the big overhanging live oak. Play for the center of the green on your approach, because water lurks to the right and, deceptively, behind the green. Take one shot at a time. Don't get upset if you miss a shot. Be patient with yourself and persevere to the end. You're getting close to home.

Daniel 3:21

And he commanded certain valiant warriors who were in his army to tie up Shadrach, Meshach, and Abed-nego, in order to cast them into the midst of the furnace of blazing fire.

A *champion* must have

the will to win

not just the *wish* to win. . . .

You have to have an *attitude* that says,

"I KNOW I can do it! And I'm GOING to *do it!***"**

PATTY BERG

Because golf is a thinking sport

more than a power sport—

unlike boxing, where

the fighter is looking for

the knockout punch—

golf rewards patient players,

who realize that they

must conquer all 18 holes

to be successful.

PETE DYE

James 1:12

Blessed is a man who

perseveres under trial;

for once he has been approved,

he will receive the crown of life,

which the Lord has promised

to those who love Him.

ENDURANCE *Produces Character*

Four qualities of a champion in golf and life are:

Be committed,

Be teachable,

Be persistent,

and Be wise.

BETSY KING

Romans 5:3–5

And not only this, but we also exult in our tribulations, knowing that tribulation brings about perseverance; and perseverance, proven character; and proven character, hope; and hope does not disappoint, because the love of God has been poured out within our hearts through the Holy Spirit who was given to us.

Pressure

BE *at* EASE

Be at ease,
do not freeze.

SAM SNEAD

Matthew 11:30

*For My yoke is easy,
and My load is light.*

Philippians 4:13

*I can do all things
through Him who
strengthens me.*

do not freeze.

Death or Glory

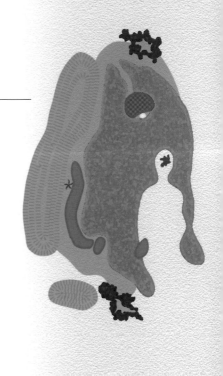

Do not come to this hole thinking "Death or glory will be my fate." It is actually one of the easier ones on the course for those who can "be at ease and not freeze." Fear itself is your greatest enemy, and the challenge of hitting your tee shot to this island green creates a snare that traps many players. The important thing is to focus on the target. It is no time to try to block out thoughts; but instead, it is a time to trust your commitment to the shot you see in your mind. When you avoid the snare of fear and reach the land, it will be easy to face the difficult putt that will likely await you.

Proverbs 29:25

The fear of man

brings a snare,

but he who trusts

in the LORD will be exalted.

THE *Real* OBSTACLE

The presence of the little white ball is the real obstacle.

It behooves any player to exercise his power over this little insignificant ball.

If this is not done, the ball will exercise its power over him.

JOHN C. HACKBARTH

HANDLING *Pressure*

You must have confidence in your ability to make the shot required.

This comes from practice.

It also comes easier after you've been in a few pressure situations and have learned to handle them.

There is no substitute for experience, and the more you learn to react properly under pressure, the better you'll be able to perform the next time.

BYRON NELSON
"Shape Your Swing the Modern Way"

1 Corinthians 2:13

. . . which things we also speak, not in words taught by human wisdom, but in those taught by the Spirit, combining spiritual thoughts with spiritual words.

MASTERY *of Fear*

To master fear, instead of dwelling on the thing feared, substitute some confidence-inspiring thought in its place. Transfer a positive attitude in place of a negative one.

Instead of thinking "I won't shoot into the bunker," think "I'll drive it down the fairway."

In place of saying to yourself "I won't slice this shot," think "I'll cover the flag all the way."

> 1 John 4:18
>
> *There is no fear in love; but perfect love casts out fear. . . .*

CHARLES MOORE
The Mental Side of Golf

In life our fear is replaced by the love of God.

You must think about what must be done to make a successful shot instead of worrying about missing it.

BYRON NELSON

Character

THE *Infallible* TEST

Golf is a test of temper, a trial of honor, a revealer of character.

DAVID FORGAN

Psalm 18:1–3

I love Thee, O LORD,

my strength.

The LORD is my rock

and my fortress

and my deliverer,

my God, my rock,

in whom I take refuge;

my shield and the

horn of my salvation,

my stronghold.

I call upon the LORD,

who is worthy to be praised,

and I am saved from

my enemies.

Homeward Bound

PAR 4 · 420 Yards

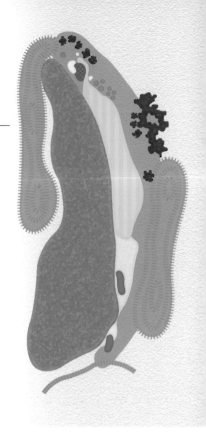

You're homeward bound. This is the final hole of The Rock. You have fought the good fight, and kept the faith. Now you must finish the course. Start with a carefully placed tee shot favoring the right side of the fairway. This sets up a difficult approach to a rather small green guarded by bunkers and water to the left. Like the game of golf itself, this hole reveals the true character of the player. If we are faithful, we will finish the course with a crown. This is not due to our performance or score, but our faith in Jesus. He is the rock-solid foundation for playing the game of life. Through Him we can finish the course of life and reach our eternal home.

2 Timothy 4:7–8

I have fought the good fight, I have finished the course, I have kept the faith; in the future there is laid up for me the crown of righteousness, which the Lord, the righteous Judge, will award to me on that day; and not only to me, but also to all who have loved His appearing.

REVELATION *of Character*

In a single round you can sum up a man, can say whether he be truthful, courageous, honest, upright, generous, sincere, slow to anger—or the reverse.

Not only is golf an excellent test of character, it is also an excellent medicament for character.

ARNOLD HAULTAIN

No other sport requires the level of integrity expected in the game of golf.

STEPHEN OLFORD

2 Timothy 2:5

If anyone competes as an athlete, he does not win the prize unless he competes according to the rules.

TEST *of* CHARACTER

Golf, my dear fellow, is the infallible test. The man who can go into a patch of rough alone, with the knowledge that only God is watching him, and play his ball where it lies, is the man who will serve you faithfully and well.

The man who can smile bravely when his putt is diverted by one of those beastly wormcasts is pure golf right through. But the man who is hasty, unbalanced, and violent on the links will display the same qualities in the wider field of everyday life.

P. G. WODEHOUSE
GOLF WITHOUT TEARS

Proverbs 4:27

Do not turn to the

right nor to the left;

turn your foot from evil

CAPTAIN *of your* SOUL

Golf is a game in which attitude of mind counts for incomparably more than mightiness of muscle.

Given an equality of strength and skill, the victory in golf will be to him who is Captain of his Soul.

Arnold Haultain
The Mystery of Golf

To control his own ball, all alone and without help or hindrance, the golfer must first and last control himself. At each stroke, the ball becomes a vital extension, an image of one's innermost self.

John Stuart Martin

> 1 Corinthians 9:25
>
> *And everyone who competes in the games exercises self-control in all things.*

God *measures us* by the CHARACTER of our *inner being*, not by what we accomplish or what we *do for Him*.

JIM SHEARD

Hole 19

REFLECTIONS *on* *Playing* THE GAME

There is great opportunity for fellowship and personal growth in the time spent with others following a round of golf. It is fun to talk about what happened. It is good to celebrate the good things and to listen empathetically to one another's woes for what went wrong. We not only need to encourage others, but we also need to encourage ourselves. We can use each experience in life and in golf as an opportunity to grow and become a better player. That is how we achieve our potential in life and in golf.

PERSONAL *Growth*

Ultimately it is not the score that counts. Instead it is the personal growth, relationship with others, character development, and faith and trust that have lasting significance in life and in golf. We need to learn to encourage each other—and to encourage ourselves—with thoughts like these:

- *Make yourself your best friend.* Be good to yourself. Encourage yourself.

- *Accept imperfection.* Acceptance will help you overcome your fear and be more consistent in your swing, scoring, and winning.

- *Don't worry about things you cannot control.*

- *Remember your good shots and your best shots.* Repeat them over and over in your mind.

- *Learn from experience.* See each experience, good or bad, as an opportunity to learn and become better.

- *Track your progress.* Watch for areas of growth or improvement even when the score may not reflect any change. Note areas that still need attention and plan your practice and strategies to improve. Especially focus on the short game as one of the quickest areas in which almost anyone can make headway.

- *Remember it is only a game!*

Apply these in the game of *life* as well.

STAY *on Course*

An endless stream of messages,
tasks and events will try
to lure us from what God
has called us to do.

As unique as God's children are,
so will be the unique experiences
that will aim to distract us
from the business at hand.

Only if we have set our priorities
and realize the significance
of what we are doing
for God's greater glory,
can we keep on keeping on.

We can then stay on course.

FRANK R. TILLAPAUGH
Unleashing Your Potential

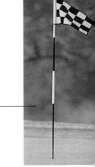

MOST *Richly* BLESSED

I asked God for strength that I might achieve.

I was made *weak* that I might learn humbly to obey.

I asked God for health that I might do greater things. I

was given *infirmity* that I might do better things.

I asked for riches that I might be happy.

I was given *poverty* that I might be wise.

I asked for power that I might have the praise of men.

I was given *weakness* that I might feel the need of God.

I asked for all things that I might enjoy life.

I was given *life* that I might enjoy all things.

I got nothing that I asked for but *everything* I had hoped for. . .

Almost despite myself my unspoken prayers were *answered.*

I am among all men most richly blessed.

UNKNOWN CONFEDERATE SOLDIER

ACKNOWLEDGMENTS

Grateful acknowledgments are made to the following:

Anderson, Steven, Senior Pastor, Bethel Church, Owatonna, Minnesota. "Maximize Your Game: Focus on Significance." Sermon outline November 17, 1996.

Armour, Tommy. *How to Play Your Best Golf All the Time*. New York: Simon and Schuster, 1953.

Berg, Patty. *The Links Letter*, Vol. 17, No. 1 (January/February 1997).

Boomer, Percy. *On Learning Golf*. London: John Lane, The Bodley Head, 1942.

Boswell, Thomas. *Strokes of Genius*. New York: Doubleday & Co., 1987.

Clampett, Bobby. *Golf Illustrated*. Quotations used with permission of Bobby Clampett and *Golf Illustrated.*

Cook, David L. Mental Advantage, Inc., 5055 Sunscape Lane South, Ft. Worth, Texas 76123, 1998.

Dye, Pete, with Mark Shaw. *Bury Me in a Pot Bunker: Golf through the Eyes of the Game's Most Challenging Course Designer*. Addison-Wesley Publishing Company, 1995. Quotations used with permission of Pete Dye.

Graham, Dr. Billy. *The Golfer's Tee Time Devotional* by James Bolly. Tulsa, Oklahoma: Honor books, 1997.

Hackbarth, John C. *The Key to Better Golf: A Mental Plan*. Madison, Wisconsin: Democrat Printing, 1929.

Haultain, Arnold. *The Mystery of Golf*. New York: Macmillan Publishing, 1910.

Hogan, Ben. "How I Hit 'Em," *Golf Illustrated* (Winter 1939).

———— *Power Golf*. New York: A. S. Barnes & Co., 1948.

Horton, Chester. "Better Golf." Unpublished booklet by the author, early 1900s.

Hutchcraft, Ron. *Peaceful Living in a Stressful World*. Nashville: Thomas Nelson, 1985.

Hyslop, Theo. *Mental Handicaps in Golf*. London: Bailliere, Tindell & Cox, 1927.

Jones, Ernest, *Swing the Clubhead*. New York: Dodd Mead, 1952.

———— "Swing the Clubhead," *Sports Illustrated and the American Golfer* (1937), and "The Swinger vs. the Hitter" (November 1937).

Jones, Bobby. *Bobby Jones on Golf* by Robert Tyre Jones, Jr. New York: Doubleday, 1966.

Kelfer, Russell. Unpublished poem, Discipleship Tape Ministries, San Antonio, Texas, 1998. Poem used with permission of the author.

King, Betsy, *The LINKS Letter*, Vol. 15, No. 2, (March/April 1995).

King, Betsey, with Scott Simpson. *US Open Champions Scott Simpson and Betsy King*, LINKS Video Series, Tape 2. Annandale, Virginia: LINKS, 1997.

Kirkaldy, Andra. *Fifty Years of Golf: My Memories*. A facsimile of the 1921 edition. Far Hills, New Jersey: United States Golf Association, 1993.

Langer, Bernhard. *The LINKS Letter,* Vol. 12, No. 3 (May/June 1992).

Littler, Gene. Original document source unknown.

Martin, John Stuart. "The Curious History of the Golf Ball" in *The Golf Quotation Book*, edited by Michael Hobbs. New York: Barnes and Noble Books, 1992.

Mitchell, Abe. *Essentials of Golf*. London: Hodder & Stoughton, 1927.

Moore, Charles. *The Mental Side of Golf*. Liveright Publishing Corp., 1929.

Nelson, Byron. "Shape Your Swing the Modern Way." *Golf Digest*, 1976.

Nicklaus, Jack. Quotations reprinted with the permission of Simon & Schuster from *Golf My Way* by Jack Nicklaus with Ken Bowden. Copyright © 1974 by Jack Nicklaus.

——— "My Favorite Lessons from Bobby Jones," *Golf Digest*, May 1989.

Olford, Stephen. Presentation to the World LINKS Conference, Callaway Gardens, Georgia, March 1996.

Padgham, Alfred. *The Par Golf Swing*. London: George Rutledge & Sons, Ltd., 1936.

Palmer, Arnold. Quotations used with permission of Arnold Palmer. Original document source unknown.

Prain, Eric M. *Live Hands*. London: Adam & Charles Black, 1946.

Runyan, Paul. *The Short Way to Lower Scoring*. A Golf Digest Book, 1979. Norwalk, Connecticut: The New York Times Company.

Saunders, Vivien. Quotation reprinted with the permission of Scribner, a Division of Simon & Schuster from *The Golfing Mind* by Vivien Saunders. Copyright © 1984 Vivien Saunders.

Schon, Leslie. *The Psychology of Golf*. London: Methuen & Co., 1922.

Snead, Sam. Original document source unknown.

Simpson, Scott. *US Open Champions Scott Simpson and Betsy King*, LINKS Video Series, Tape 2. Annandale, Virginia: LINKS, 1997.

Taylor, J. H. *Taylor on Golf*. D. Appleton & Co., 1903.

Tillapaugh, Frank R. *Unleashing Your Potential: Discovering Your God-Given Opportunities for Ministry*. Ventura, California: Gospel Light/Regal Books, 1988.

Travis, Walter J. "Building Up a Game, VII—The Swing," *American Golfer,* October 1920.

Venturi, Ken. Original document source unknown.

Wodehouse, P. G. *Golf Without Tears*. New York: George H. Doran, 1919.

JIM SHEARD & WALLY ARMSTRONG

*Wally Armstrong (l) &
Jim Sheard (r) Continue
to enjoy playing the game.*

JIM SHEARD has a Ph.D. in organizational behavior and has been an executive and consultant for more than twenty-five years. He now devotes his time to writing and speaking on the parallels between golf, life, and faith. Jim is an avid amateur golfer with a handicap in the mid-teens and a desire to improve. In 1997 he and Wally Armstrong co-authored the bestseller *In His Grip.* It has encouraged countless people in their life, faith, and golf. Golf fellowship groups have formed, using it and the study guide as the framework for their time of study together.

WALLY ARMSTRONG competed in more than 300 PGA Tour events worldwide, gaining a lifetime membership to the PGA Tour. In his first Master Tournament, Wally finished just three strokes behind Gary Player, setting a record rookie score of 280. While serving as a caddie for such legendary figures as Gary Player, Wally heard Billy Graham use analogies from golf to teach spiritual truths from the Bible. As a golf instructor, Wally put this to use in his videos, clinics, and books on golf.

Jim and Wally's combined experience as tour player, instructor of golf, golf historian, educator, organizational psychologist, and executive give them valuable and varied perspectives. They share a common desire to encourage others in the games of life and golf.

For information on:

Ordering Study Guides for

In His Grip and Playing the Gar

Starting a Golf Fellowship or

Study Group

Hosting a Golf Event or Clinic

Subscribing to our Newsletter

Other resources for golfers on

life and faith

Contact In His Grip Resources:

P.O. Box 642

Owatonna, MN 55060-0642

1-888-899-GRIP or 1-507-455-3377

www.in-his-grip.com